counting to
DIWALI

A CELEBRATION IN NUMBERS

Written by S.C. Baheti
Illustrated by Rohan Dahotre

ISBN 978-1-63683-009-4 (pbk.)
ISBN 978-1-63683-991-2 (ebook)

Printed in the United States of America

DIWALI

Diwali is known as the festival of lights and it marks the return of Lord Rama following his defeat of Ravanna, the 10-headed demon king, as well as the end of his 14 years in exile. On this "no moon night" clay lamps (diyas) lit the night sky, so that Rama and his followers could find their way home.

Today in India, and across the world during Diwali, lights are strung from houses and in the streets, as well as small lamps, to light up the night, in an echo of the night of Rama's triumphant return. Diyas are lit and sweets are enjoyed by all. Diwali is celebrated by many people in many different ways and it marks a special time of year for family and friends to gather and celebrate together.

Do you celebrate Diwali? What special celebrations do you enjoy with your family?

1

EIK

one

Rangoli

traditional colorful design

2

DOH

two

Jhumke

earrings

3

TEEN

three

Kandil
colorful lanterns

4

CHAR
four

5

PANCH

five

upahaar

festive gifts

6

CHE

six

7

SAAT

seven

Phool maala

flower garlands

8

AAHT

eight

Diya
lamps

9

NOU

nine

Phulzhadi
sparklers

10
DUS
ten

Laddoo

sweets

1-EIK   2-DOH

3-TEEN   4-CHAR

5-PANCH 6-CHE

7-SAAT   8-AAHT

9-NOU   10-DUS

KEEP COUNTING

CPSIA information can be obtained
at www.ICGtesting.com
Printed in the USA
LVHW072246230821
695909LV00002B/200